A City Sky at Night
Volume 2 of Dark cloud White cloud Dusk Sandstone

Paul Fearne

chipmunkapublishing
the mental health publisher

Paul Fearne

All rights reserved, no part of this publication may be reproduced by any means, electronic, mechanical photocopying, documentary, film or in any other format without prior written permission of the publisher.

> Published by
> Chipmunkapublishing
> United Kingdom

http://www.chipmunkapublishing.com

Copyright © **Paul Fearne 2018**

ISBN   978-1-78382-434-2

A City Sky at Night

What is there
Is not there

And when we have finished
There will be a long pause
And then
To be the gatherer of rose petals

I have not seen the belief we have
In some time
But that is not a worry
We have the chance to be
And be in

And here
Where the fathomable
Meets the sea
There will be a small temperance
That seeks itself in ardour
Be the chance
And you will have a gift

When the night begins
And the daylight recedes
There will be hope
And all that will come to pass

What do we say?
When wheeling and healing
Enter the fray

What is there to do?
When the noise departs
And the speed increases

The listening we do to sense things aright
Is here
And when it is here
All manner of things are good

To this we march on
Onto the cauldron

Paul Fearne

That has no fire
And no earth
To file the linear
And the bold

Be in the making
And you will have a hearth
Be now
Or peace be yours

There is a mass of things
That require doing
But here
There is only one
Only one thing that needs doing
And that is to give hope
And to that
We must add
To be
In the most inconceivably ungainly way
And here
We will love
And know love
And feel love
And do the things that instil it
And love from the depth
And from the shallow
From the in
And the out
And when we feel inclined
To be one with love
That is my hope
And a hope that lingers
Why is this a seeming impossibility?
Who knows
But with folly
It might just work!

And here
Where the sand between our toes
Is enough
To keep us flying

A City Sky at Night

There will be the dance
And all that will be

The climbing we do
To set the dream ablaze
Is enough to hope upon hope
And when we are near
And not far
There will be an event
That has no equal
And here
The sentential belief
Will be enough
To fathom a mighty abyss
The next thing we know
We are there
And we will know
What it is like to sing
And be in tune
With so much

And here
Where the sands of the hour
Touch that little deeper
There will be nothing left to speak of
Only what is in keeping with the clouds

The sense we have
That the tempest is not just another view
Of the same thing
We must not tarry
We must only come for what is there
And here
Where we linger nightly by the fuse
There is only the recompense of the stars
What have I said?
But all that is
What have I said?
But what is now
Be true
And this will solve all
Be true

Paul Fearne

And the next time we have an adventure
It will be as if nothing had happened
And then
And only then
Respite
And the dreams of dragonflies

There are places
And then there are places
I have been to that place
Where there is nothing
And here I derive my strength
To carry on
To new places
That are untold
I have no fear
Because of that
And when the night descends
I will be ready
And here
Where nightingales have their say
There will be a time to rejoice
And a time for levity

What will become of us
In the time between this word and the next
Here
Where I lie in wait
I will have the sense to go on achieving
Doing that which is amazing
And here
I will have no notion
Of this
Or that
Or all that is
And when we stop
Well
What then?

Sometimes the dark clouds part
And the sunlight comes through
And all is well for that briefest of moments

A City Sky at Night

And here where I sing
I sing for us
I sing for the day
And the night
And of course
I sing for the twilight
And when there is nothing left
There is a new kind of wanting
It nestles up to us
Like a dream
And when we need more
We will have it
Be the one that binds itself to the raft
And you will have many adventures
Many things to occupy your time
And then
When we see things aright
There will be
Something we will never miss

The well is in the garden
The fate is in the hill
Where there is more of light
Dark will have its fill

There can only be what we have in stall
And here
Where light wins
There will be a new need to be
And a way to try to outwit ourselves

The sense I have
That never a person has had
Is to be the unnerved
At the slightest beck and call

And here
Where the trees are not in unison
There will be a chance to feel anew
And a chance to be that thing
Which has as its base

Paul Fearne

The couriers of happenstance
As they wind their way through the air
And into tomorrow

What can never be
Will never be
And here
Where the closest insistence
Needs a new timing
There will be more to fill us
With wholesome laughter

What we have said
Is not enough
And yet it is enough
In the pause between acceptances
What we say
Is like a time to be
And a time to want
And a time to be wholesome
And just a time
That never fails

The trust we place in the stars
Is enough to keep the mist in motion
And here
Where the need we have is no longer
There will be more than we could have hoped

There will be time to see anew
And when we do
Very good

And now the journey really begins

In the mist
In the forest
In every conceivable lining
Of this or that jacket
There lies a fathoming want
And here
Where it is time to see the warmth

A City Sky at Night

Come off an effortful chest
There can be nothing more than this
Nothing in the seam of things
Nothing in the in-between of things
Nothing in the round-abouts
Or the ups-and-downs
That will drag me away from this
And here
Where we have died those thousand deaths
There will be a chance to repatriate our souls
And now long for something new
That new is a journey
That new is a fathoming desire
That lasts as long as it can
And when we are through
Complete release
Of this or that

What we see in the margins
Is more than we thought possible

And here
Where the strangeness of the dream
Begins to palpitate
There will be a time for rejoicing
And a time for letting go

I have felt
In the middle of it all
A sort of weight lifting
But then a return
To all that is

When we rush
There is more to say
When we fear
There is a country for the deliverance
Looking in the midst of the tread
There is a fathoming mass
That heralds
As it harks

Paul Fearne

Be the tune
I implore you

What is there left to dream
Now that the new need is upon us?
There are flecks and guesses
And all that will be

And here
Where the nuances of a thousand nights labour
Bring the darkness of a thousand unheard murmurs
There will be a tune on the lips of the sea
And she will right herself
And be that thing that does not bite

This thing is in all of us
And it stills us to the core
And here
Where we bleed the deepest
There will be wishing
And all that is

What do we say
When the blood is away?
What do we mean
When the room is all clean

What have I said
To be in the front?
I have said all that matters
And all that is

And here
Where the fathoming mist lies dormant
There will be a larger calling
It is a calling that straddles faith
And has the news of millions
At its base

What is in the dreaming
Is near at hand
What is in the song

A City Sky at Night

Is like so much

And here
Where the testament is dissolved
There will be time to be
And withhold all niceties
This much is true
And this much will be
And all will have its day
And all will be in the light
And all will be
And all will be

There is a chance
That it will rain
But the chance is not large
And we are free of all that mists

The thing that binds
Is the same thing that releases

And here
Where we dance no more
There will be chances
To raise the belly of forgiveness
And have it settle on us in unison

There is the thought
That this is a deserted island
With only one of us here
But that is not a truth
It is more like an ocean of beings
That linger by our graves
And then raise us up
The wanting we have
To a new sphere
And a larger way of being

Be sure of yourself

What is there
More to say?

Paul Fearne

What is there
More to do?
We have no recourse to the stars
And here
Where the treading on water
Is a thing to be guarded
There will be a mighty release
And a still mightier
Need to be and yet be strong

I have not the feelings of a soldier
But I am one
I have not the tread of a warrior
But I am one
What we see now
Is not in the harvest
Nor in the moon
Here what we say
Is 'Now!' and be done with it
What have I got but all
What have I got
But nothing
I sense you are near
It could be that my senses are awry
And you are far
We shall see

What is here
My faithful?
I have found a song
To play to you
It is a song of dark forgiveness
And has as its time
The withering of nuances

Like me
I say
Like me
There is nothing to quell the ancient tune
Nothing more to do than be in amidst it
And see the quell
And fathomless void

A City Sky at Night

Intransigent of sight
Forever alight
Never seeing the day
But only the night
I see this round
As a sort of deliverance per se
And know that
When things arise
They will be blistered
From their own exertion

What do we say
When the tempest is at its height?
We say nothing
But do
We have what is most precious
And lo it is found
And here where the sentience
Of things past
Is near at hand
There will come a reckoning
That is for fools
And troubadours
And here
Where we get our most ardent pleasure
There will be a recompense
And a new need to fly

What have the doves of delight
Given the sea?
There is no way of telling
And know way of knowing
Put we persist
And lower our eyes
Be the past
And ruin will be yours
Be the future, and slowly you will perish
Be the present
And all will be yours

What is the remorse?
It is for life

Paul Fearne

What is the recompense?
It is everything
And here
Where we love to be
There is nothing more
It is only the sands we must watch
But what of this?
It is nothing other than ourselves
As we pinion forwards
In concentric circles
That give life
As they give forever

The new need
Is here
It shocks
As the birds of flight shock
There is a way forward
But it is hard
It is black
As it is night
It is lo
And it is found

What we do believe
Is that the sun will rise tomorrow
But is this the certainty we seek?
Yes
And no
And here
We look into the folds
And see ourselves
Resting here
With lifelong adherence
And love in its yoke

Be the thing that clears
And the sight of our endeavours
Will be a mighty harvest
And when we know
What to do with ourselves
We will launch again

A City Sky at Night

For the sails, as for the ships

What we most must do
Is saddle up for the journey
And have it reach its inner strength
I am with you compassion
Through my tread is weak

That furious storm
That enters as in night
Has all the listing of the feather
And all the flight
Of the morrow
In touch with all?
We should hope
And here
Where we enter in dreams untold
There will come a night
That has no insolence
And no belief in the things to come

What of this?
Which way do we turn?
When the barrow has run its full course
There will be more
Than all the trappings
And all the nuances
To that speed
And that way of turning
We will be
Like never before
And here
Where sand is of the aching
We will touch
And our hands will let go
And all that will be left
Will be the tempest
And her raging sea

Beware
There is no tomorrow
It is a fantasy

Paul Fearne

That has only belief to blame
Come now
We must not worry
We must only couch our plans in wool
And have the need we have demolished
And then set aright
Amongst the stars
And all their strength
Be a martyr
And there will be a cost
Be a wastrel
And there will be a cost
Be a deliverer of news
And there will be no cost
To you
Or the rest of us
Just be
Let us see

What is this now?
The sense has raised its head
And the feelings of remorse
Are in the middle of a fairway
Do the thing which keeps you still
Is the same thing
That treasures the night
Be here
I hear you say
Be here
And there will always be a place for you
And when we are through
The night will play a solemn march
And it will be for the soldiers amongst us
And when we dive
We dive for us all
And here
Where the meeting place of two hearts be
There will be enough time
To shadow in the chalice
And here
Be in tune with the sea
As it bends its way around the sun

A City Sky at Night

As the sun rises in unison with all
Be a harper
In a harpers land
And there will be much to be thankful for

Be the tune
On the lips of sea
And there will be life

And when we have
The silence we need
There will be a remedy
That cures all

And here
Where the newness of a fading sun
Is at its lowest ebb
New whisperings
And ancient ties
Will be all we need
To end what is un-endable
This is what we say
To the chosen
As they march
Once again
Out of sight

Be the wind
I implore you
You will find all
And all will find you

The cause is deep
But the rewards are endless
And here
Where we find ourselves
The furthest
There will come a mighty cry
That senses what is to come
And here
Where life beats its fullest
There is a new feeling

Paul Fearne

That belies the rest

What we need now
Is to rest
There will be much time for frivolity
When the sun sets
And when we come for it
There will never be a moment like it
To win
A mighty battle
And have as our rest
The feelings of great repour
The glow a magnificent sheen
A sheen for the ages
And when we are done
And when we are done
Yes
This much
And more

The difference
In meaning
From this word
To the next
Is a comfort
And a joy
To all those
Who wish to be in the driver's seat
Of this carriage
To the next
Be one
 To say
"I am here"
And then wait
What you will find
Is something
Immune
From the tenacity of a voice
That has no shod to shoe
And no feeling to find

Be the one who laughs

A City Sky at Night

And you will laugh loudest

There is never enough time
There is never enough time
There is always enough time
If we wait
And if we sing
Our loudest song
And here
Where desire is in the morning
There will be more than we could have hoped
I love
What it is that we say
When all seems lost
We query our lineage
And know
That time will not forget us
And then
When we are on our knees
Deliverance
And all that shall come to pass

The noise we make as children
Is the noise of the centuries
It whistles more than ever
Do you remember it
Your voice
Your nearing years
We have all
Right here

There are here
Music's of the mind
Whose dance upon the fray
Has us all carried away

I am one to listen
To all that is
What I hear
Is enough to fill a stadium
Of heart felt wanting
And moon danced stomping

Paul Fearne

There is a place
That has no fear
There is a place
That looks for echoes
It is our place
And we search for something more
And do not shirk the 'more'
As mere meanderings

The time it takes
To rattle these bones
Fills us with empathy
And all that is good

What do we have of sorrow?
Is it not the thorn which binds?
Is it not the tempest that lashes?
We hear not of such things
Here in the wilderness
We grimage for each step
And we fossil for untold need
And here
Where the trees of undulating directness
Feel their cavernous graduation
All the more quietly still
Here
Where we bind ourselves to the raft
There is more than can be said
I am the one who carries
I carry water for our needing
And long distance waits for our caravan
What is more
I wait for no known sentinel
As he breaks stride in front of us
Here I will come
And know that life is for the endless
And tears are from the makeshift
There can be nothing else
Only what is
And what is not

A City Sky at Night

There are no plans for intermission
There are no plans for what is in us already
There are plans for the basking of sun
And the tremulous insistence of the stars

Here
Where the nursing of tears peaks
There will come a night time stranger
That has as his ears
The turpentine of the waves
What of this?
It is of no regard
Or no remorse
Be glad
There is something to do
And here
Where the sand is at its outer most visage
There will come time
To harbour a new delivery
That fathoms as it up takes
And delivers in full regalia
Here we will see ourselves
In ragamuffin behove
There can be nothing more insistent
And nothing more
Well
Intransigent

What we dream of
When we are awake
Is the dream of life
And love
And all that will come to pass
I am here
Where mistletoe lingers
I am here
Where the sounds of the hour glass sing
I am here
Where never before whisperings of the night reverberate
I am here
Where the distance doesn't matter
I am here

Paul Fearne

Where angels sometimes dream
I long for here
And now
And all that will come
And what is more
There is a chance to be
And be told
And lye
And built a fence against the wind
Here
Oh here

What in the name of the fiddle is this?
It is all we ever hoped for
It is something more
As it is something less
We can dream
But to dream
Is not to be
To dream
Is in essence
To write
This is a dream
That has severity as its heart
That has seamless wonder as its breast
What is more
We have a wish for more
But what is that?
I hear you say
Be quiet now
There will be a chance to walk
And tell the stranger
That light is coming
That what will cure is coming
That what can never be
And subsequently always be
Is coming
We will see
And then bring it along

The mess
Is now gone

A City Sky at Night

What is left
Is the all or nothing of fate
What we see
Can never be rendered
Into any art
Produced by any person
In any time
But here
And now
And this
Is what we all dream of
Not just us writers
Not just our artists
Not just our poets
But everyone
Who has ever broached a net
Who has ever sung the song
Who has ever been tutored by greatness

And here
We simply be
And let be again
Where is the 'to be'?
Where is the sound that rings?
Where is the news of the world
Except in our sleep?

There are never times to fight
And this is one of those times
We must relinquish our hold on being
And jump into the fray
But we must acquiesce to fate
And be driven by her

The story of the multitudes
Is told here
The story of what it takes
To win the cup
And be the one who wins
Instead of just reading about it
There is more to be told here
But for now we are content

Paul Fearne

Be the sand between the toes of your sweet
Be the one who finishes last
But has the greatest story to tell

There are things to be learnt
In all games
And here we have it in spades
'the learning of the learned!'

And I say something here
'It matters not what afflicts you
'As long as you have a witticism at hand
'And a story to relate afterward!'

There you go then
Something for the ages

Something to take home at least, on this, your mighty adventure

Be the withering
On the branch
And you will fall
Be the fruit
On the branch
And you shall find a mighty acceptance
What is more
There is more
There is more coming
In the middle of things
We will wait
And know that life is for laughter
And kites are for flying
Who do we need here?
We need ourselves
And ourselves only

The withering of ancient monastery vines
Has nothing left to give
What we bleed for
Is more than we can hope

A City Sky at Night

What is this thing, hope?
Is it a thing that keeps us going?
Yes
Is it a thing that holds us back?
No
What do we fear from it then?
It is untold dimensions
That seek redress
That have us as a starlit companion
And here
Where we grab hold of hope the tightest
There is nothing more that can be done
What is envisaged
Is more than hope has hoped
Be in the margin
And truisms will escape their mark
Be well
'I hear you'
Be well
And we all will be with you

Where are we?
I hear you ask
We are in the never
The never and the begone
There are times
Just as there are places
That have in themselves
The niceties
Of a thousand night's laughter
And here
Where we sing no more
There is a chance to breath
And have the shoding taken from our feet

What do we catch with?
The soles of our feet
The soul of an athlete?
Yes
And here we cast a glimpse at everything
There is only one thing missing

Paul Fearne

And that is us
As we climb again
To that misty harbour
That is a place of rest for a brief time
And then onward
And through

What we have
Is a new need
A need to fathom the abyss
And here
Where the languishing
Of sandstone is enough
To fill the ready invective
There will be recompense
And all that is want
To be given
By the sands that hold us

I live by the hour
Nay
By the second
My merit is in the changing
Of this fate
To the next

My love is that which is gone
But I don't wish anymore
For the love that is imperfect
I wish only for the whole
The whole of life
Not to be diminished
By this or that fault

When we see things in the right way
We see things in the right way
What way is this?
It is up
As it is down
It is roundabouts
It is there
What we see

A City Sky at Night

Enlivens the world
And what we see
Gives sustenance
To the sea

What is this
That gives life as it takes?
It is nothing other than ourselves
As we fight once again
For the taking of water
From the clouds
To the sea
And then to let go of it
And see it whence it came
The life in between
Is nothing other
That the signature of the morrow
As she fights again
For the stillness of life

What do we have before us?
It is the journey
And we are the supplicants
It is the rite of Spring
As we are its demands
Surety gives milk
But sand has no ilk
And where the newness of the sky
Has its chance at average
We will dance higher
And more swift
And gain that foothold
That is surety in this life
What life is this?
It is the life of the multitude
That has broken into several fragments
And knows itself to be the one who knows
And there
Then
In the night
Dreams
And the wakefulness of everybody

Paul Fearne

As we search for something more
And something less
And whatever we don't have

What is this thing
That has right as it does belief?
There is a never ending graduations here
As there is in everything
And here
Where we nestle in at night
There are changes that have no ilk
This is what we have fought so hard for
Yes
And to say the least
Yes
What we have fought for is the never ending
And here
Where life comes to completion
There is nothing other than silk
Silk where there was once sand
We know
That when the seeds of the larger turning
Are given roster
There is more than enough to keep
And here
In the meantime
There is a lucky stance
That believes itself to be truth
What have we sought for then?
All, and then again some

What is left
Of the afterglow?
It is diminished
In compunction
To this
O this
And here
Where light never fades
There will be exposure to the elements
That have no time
To rustle into fairy tales

A City Sky at Night

And here
Where sand is replaced by steel
(Our souls are made of this stuff)
There will be all we could have hoped for
In traipsing
In narrowing
In the needing of arrows of light
To see us through
There is wholesome delight
And ugly witching
There is the way forward
As there is the way back
Love the adventure
It will love you back
But before you become stuck
Nomenclature for beginners

What can there be
But the wind as it flies to you?
What can there be
But tethers of delight
That hold importance like a gemstone?
I know of nothing other
That turning inside and out
To be the one that gets to you
And all that you have left

The forest is a single tree
That harbours all that we know
'The Known World' indeed
And here
Where the caustic mess is like a missive from the determinant
O here
There is at stake nothing less than all
What if we have no means to fight?
We shall build them
Out of the nothing we have become
And then, once built, we will join the battle of our souls
And let the movement carry us forward
To wear we want to go
What is this, I hear you ask

Paul Fearne

It is all, and then some

What we need
Is to start again
Without the wanna-be may-be
Kind of speight between things
That we see in other walks

I have seen this much
That when the branches
Of the tree of knowledge
Are out stretched
To their COMPLETE limit
There is a noise that can be heard
It is the noise of you and me
As we creep around
An abandoned abbey
And the sound
Of the light going through
The stained glass
And here
Where we sit now
Is past all adventure
Of every kind
Except this
And that
And everything in between

What is in the mix
Is not
Here, nor there
But withheld
By nuances of fate
We feel them
And have our chance at hearing
But the rough is no more
No more on the wind
And on the sky

What lies ahead
Is already in us
What we never knew

A City Sky at Night

Was like the wind
The wind that believes itself
To be alive

What the mountain also knew
Is not what we are more likely to stall upon
But what we are less likely to see as our own
Be one
I hear you pronounce
Be two
I hear you say
Be three
And they all came in a rush
So there you are

Wishing
And wanting
Wishing
And wanting
There is a chance
To believe in all
And that chance is now
I have found a ready window
Under the fox turn relic

What do you say
To this?
What do we all say?
It is here
The night time
And here
Is what remains of us
There is turpitude
In the mass
And the rite of fire
To be delighted by

There is one small thing remaining
It is life
And all she will bring

The land beneath our feet

Paul Fearne

Does not shift
The land beneath our feet
Always shifts

What is there
Is not there

What we see
In the land above
Is the seeing of dreams

The mistletoe is what holds us

The dreams of a sailor

The dreams of every sailor to sail the sea

What can be
And what will be

There is now time to see
The sea
And rise above our challenges
And see the feelings of larger people

What is it
That lifts us
Higher
And higher
Into the expanse of blue that is the beyond

It is here
On this piece of land
We can touch it
And feel it
And have on it
All that we have ever wanted

The newness of the fading sun
Is enough to embellish triumph
With all the rose can give

A City Sky at Night

What we say when the rose has finished
Is enough to still us to the core
And here
Where we love and be loved
A new horizon
That sings as it lets sing
And a new way to be
That has none of the after
And more of the pre

The distance
Between this beat of a heart
And the next
Is enough
To tailor our necessities
To be within reach of the dawn

And here
Where we fall back
To safe ground
There is a need
We have
To break out
Of our mould
And see ourselves
Once again
Alert
And alive
And here
Where we signal for the fire
And have let go of the water
There is a new found belief
That things will right themselves
Of their own accord
Of there being buoyed
By mists undiminished

The dream
It carries us
In new directions
And in new ways to be

Paul Fearne

What is left of the old
Is left
And here
Where we find a thing that is mightier
Than life itself
We find solace
And the things
That troubled us
Are no longer there

Be in tune with life
There is much to be said
And much that will
Fathom
A mighty form

Distances
They matter so much
We don't know what
To do with ourselves

The testing of trees
In the wind
Is more than we had ever hoped for

The dreams we have
To say farewell
Are not here

What the treasure of the night
Is longing to be
Is not enough to sustain us

The forest
Is
In itself
A wonder
That has life
Despite the
Longing
Of the trees

A City Sky at Night

The never before
Known
Dream
Is the one we encounter
Most frequently

The tempest
This much has been said
But what of its allure?
Can we really find comfort
In its embrace?
Yes
And
Of course no

Here
And there
We find something to rest our head on
Here
And of course
There
We know where to put our future
We keep it for keepsakes
And have the never ending tide
As our heart

When we dream
Here we love
When we dream
Here we find solace
The dream
The dream
What is in the weave
Is the question we must ponder
The weave
Of things

And here
Where the silence has only rapture
There is a noise
That lingers on

Paul Fearne

We must use this noise
To create
And in shaping reality
There will be change

What now?
Who can say
There will be much to do
And much to be

Family
Is in our hearts
Can we live
When niceties are thick
And rambling feelings
Walk with newfound aplomb

The withering on the vine
Is no more

The steps we take to solve ourselves
Is enough to bend the bridge of now
And carry us forward
And into what awaits

Here
O here
There is enough life
To fill a catacomb
And when we sing
We sing for others
But for ourselves as well
And before we are there
There will be labour of a thousand days
That dreams of silken ash have never seen

And now
We linger on
Feeling to parting as never before
And here
Where silk derives from ash
And the distance from the sun to here

A City Sky at Night

Is like a volcano
There will be time to act
And time to be one
With all that is

Having the courage.

Being in belief.

Signing on.

Watering the sky with our tears.

Hatching the yards to go.

Finding what is left.

Having more that we had hoped.

What the dress is here to say.

The nearness of it all.

The science of clouds

Starburst, and reconciliation.

What the fingers do because of our affliction.

Wanting, and having.

We march onward
Despite the curse which is existence
We march towards the gates
Of the drawbridge
And in nearing them
Hear the sounds of the other side
They are light
With humour
And song
And happiness

Paul Fearne

The treasures of the well-spring
Are enough to be in transit
They rub
Against the rub
And have soil for heals
Much is here
In times of well-ness
Much that can only be described as good
But when we see ourselves
In the mirror of the times
We see the good
And its wings
They land things upright
And have the dimensions of all things

There are times
In amongst it
That we wish we never were
But what keeps us going?
Pure courage
And here
Where the sand between our toes
Is the thing that is most important
There will come a light
It is the light of our forbears
Who went through things too
And when we are through
A mighty release
And when it is time
To feel such things
We must continue
To live
And breathe
And know our spot
Is not the one we live for
We go forward
And up
And through
And then
Well
We all must see this for ourselves

A City Sky at Night

What is left of our ease
Is enough to fill a lake
Half full
The other half
Full of dreams
And antidotes

And here
Where the fashion is to deride
We will buck the trend
And know ourselves to be safe

What is new
Is not old
What is here
Is now
And what gathers us
Into folds of night
And then lets us go
Is the need of the stars
To have friendship
And all that can be
And all that can be

What we have left
Is all

The lightest flight
The sense to make it
All intensive

What the noise will give to us
Is not what we can deliver
We must keep it
And have the stars gives us more
More than we can have
And then get a good night sleep
And start again

The distance between this dream and the next
Is what the wind has gauged as its own

Paul Fearne

And when we shout
We shout for the daylight
And we shout
Just to pass the time
And we shout
For always being last
And we shout
For the chance to be
And be with a solid 'B'

This much is sure
We can find ourselves in the darkness
And find what is never enough

Belong
Belong somewhere
Belong in the field
Belong in the day
Belong in the night
Just say where you are going
And that you will be there

The moisture from the clouds
Is not enough to sink us
The rain that comes
Comes in miniatures
Compared to what we can bare
You see
We have been there
And know what strength is
Strength to be
And strength to write
And strength to be the one who says 'yes'
And carry us forward
Into times unknown
And times less reckoned
By the brush
And the rub

The dreams are here
The test is here

A City Sky at Night

And what we have found
Is that when we drew a bow
The sounds of autumn
Were enough to be what is here

Don't fend
Off
This little piece of delight
We need our friends to remain true
And here
Where the sand is not in proportion
There is something we have forgotten to do
We have forgotten to wash
This hand
Or that
This far
Or that far
And here
Where we have no light
We may find ourselves
In that greater majesty
That is the sky
What have we felt?
But all

The nice
And the bland
And everything that sets us apart
From all the memories
Of a thousand nights
Hunger
And a thousand nights steel

What is there left of us
What is there
To say
We have found much
But how much more
Is there to be found?
We will see in the wind
And in the middle of it
The middle of what?

Paul Fearne

The middle of the river of course
And there is nothing more to find?
What can we say
That we have not already said?
Nothing
But we must continue
And in that
Record our journey
So that it may be repeated as a formula
Amongst the stars

What is the beautiful
And why is it here?
We say to ourselves
Over and over again

But the need we have to live
Concords all insistences
And then
When the last of faith
Has had its say
There will be more than we ever hoped
This is what we say
To the end
We say 'transmute your guile'
And it does
And we go there
To where we want to be
And here
There is a dream
That has nothing other
Than reality at its base
Come and be stronger
Than the wind
You will live a hardy life
But your rewards will be endless

What is left of our ease?
It is here
In fragrance
And in heart

A City Sky at Night

What we say
When there is nothing left to say
What we feel
When there is nothing left to feel

Solemn times
And ridges of regrets
The regrets of dragonflies
Or so it seems

And here
Where laughing is for the times
There is a little piece of the real
That holds everything in place

The foreknowledge of a stranger
Has us all perplexed
There is nothing more we can do
But ride the wild sea
And cast our visage
Into marble arches

What we see in the mist
Is all that is
What we see in the mist
Is the shadow of you and me
What we see in the mist
Is the longing we have
This longing
Sustain us
And in the end
It's sweet embrace
Leaves us
And we come to where we are now
And that is in the burrow
And on the windswept peak
And here
O here
There is nothing of the good
And the bad
Nothing of the flight in the night
Here

Paul Fearne

O here
There is integrity of action
That leads to unified belief
That leads to peace
And calm
And the desire to be

What we have seen
In the dead of night
Is nothing other
Than all
Nothing other than
The windswept peak
As it shudders up to the centre
And then
Releases
We are not attuned to combat
What fate has in store for us
But what we say
When the dawn is in the hills
Holds much weight
Even with fate
The levity of the situation fills us
And lifts us
And guides us home
Till we have had our fill
Our fill of what?
Our fill of adventure?
No we will never tire of that
Our fill of need?
Perhaps so
If that is what it takes
So be it

The times
They are fathoming the deep
They are listening to the night
They hear
What is said
In times of despair
They hear
What is bold

A City Sky at Night

And lengthened
In sight

Be bold yourself
Be the one who tries
And who wins
The mighty prize
As if by magic

There are wantings
That fear not to tread
On any surface
Of any plane
Are here
Where life is at its fullest
There is respite
From all the goings on
Of this life
And the next

What do we fear?
When the night is here?
There is nothing to fear
And nothing to run from
There is only
The wishing of great aunts
To burn a candle
And here
Where we must do our duty
There comes a certain solace
Perchance
A dream?
What is this I hear you say?
A dream?
Yes a dream
I am one to believe
And not to sway
Not to sway out of the way
For in time
In guessing time
There is the silence I need
To help me finish this work

Paul Fearne

And be the one who
Drinks the draught
The potion of love
That sustains us all

The potion of love
I had it once
It was quite a beverage
But it didn't live up to expectations
The love interest went
Of her own accord
Or was she pushed
I never can tell
I was distraught
But I found my calling
And now I write
To save myself from the abyss
Now I write
That is what I do

It is like I had never had love
But I must say
It was nice to experience it
Even though it didn't last
My career got in the way!
It's like there is a new beginning
A reset has been called
What can I say is here?
The heady days
They are back again
And here we go
One two three....

One two three....
Here we go!
Yes this is the right way
And not the wrong way
Believe in the feeling
Is it love?
Or is it work?
The choice is yours

A City Sky at Night

Never speak of these things
Again
But yes you can
You see
These things are open for discussion
I think that is a natural way to act
Yes, yes, come now, we must not get lost
Lost we will be if we continue
But we must continue
Yes we must, it is true
It is true alright
Come on then let us go
Yes
Let us go
We will see many things
On this grand adventure
Don't you think?

When we raise a glass
There will be nothing left
Of this or that
Or any of it

And here
Where the sands of the hour glass
Sink in time to a new muse
There will be refurbishments to be made
And long lunches to be had

What is more
There is never a time that we have had
That hasn't listed on the shores of newness
And here
Where we lounge for the sake of the good
There is no time to waste
We are here now
And here
Means also
And in the long run
A treasure
You will be bold

Paul Fearne

When we are free
Ah, then
The sky will blister like a tomb
And we will have the need of the newborn
Without the resistance to be

Be here
Oh life
Be the one that shines
In the grave
And in the stars

The testament to this
Is that life is for giving away
And when we can see
The cat from the tail
We will know
A mighty thing

And here
Where life measures itself in ounces
There will be more time for us
And then less time for the lonesome
Despite our fondness

What have the sands said
That makes us shy so?
The thing that does set us free
Is not what you would expect
It is something deep within us
But then again not
It is something in the wind
But then again not
It is something that we can only see in the dark
And then
When we have finished all our searching
There will come a place
And a chance to be placated

Where do we search
Oh enlivened soul?
Where do we search

A City Sky at Night

When the search seems endless?
We search in our hearts
That much is true
We search in our being
And all that will come to pass

What is this, but all
What is this, but null
What can we say of it
It is over there
Beyond the fence
In the garden
And through

What have we left
But the fathoming of enterprise
What have we to know
But the threads of heart beat entwined

There is a saying
I know not its origin
Or its content
But what it says is harrowing
It says
We are….
And then today
The vapour rises
And what is in need
Is the longed for journey
One that takes us far
And back again
And around
And through
And then
The in-between
Of corsetry
And contumely
Here
For a final say

There is a touch of something new
I have heard it said

Paul Fearne

That the rhyme that meters
Bores
But what I will say to you
Is that there are chances in the semblance
Of things transpired
And things belittling nature

What can we have
But all
What can there be
But the withstanding of night

The need we have
To belittle the stars
Is not enough
To fend of fate

There is a chance
To be the distance
There is a chance
To feel what is right

I am new here
But I have heard it said
Many times
We will win
And we will!

What is there too this?
When the wind and the rain
Conspire
To shift our noble height
There will be more to come
And then
When light and ease have a bashful
There is nothing to it!

The trembling of sense
And noisome grief
Is laden withal and without

And here

A City Sky at Night

Where we chance our arm
One more time
There is licentious talk
Of wanting to have
What cannot be had

And when we wind
We do so with tethers
And then at ease
Soaked in feathers

And here we are
But where is that?
It is the rind of life
But where is that?
It is further from any shore
Known
But will we come back?
It is up to the gods
Only they can fathom the scene
But is that tricky?
Immeasurably so
But should we wait?
Yes, we all should
But can we come?
No, it is inconceivable
But wait
There is still time
To bastion our lovings
And have them ride with us
Along winding roads
Byways and highways
Lashing ourselves to the mast
So we can hear the sirens song

Come now
We must be quick

What is love?
I have heard it sung that it is a thing to be avoided
The sparks
The waiting

Paul Fearne

The doubt
The amazement
The enslavement
The great feelings
Is this love?
May it cast itself upon me
And I will find out

And here
Yes here
There are nuances to be sure
Nuances in feeling
And life
And the distance between us all

What can we say
When the noon is at the aft
When portals are precise
And dreams are there ebullient
Come now, and be the tree
And we will look after you

The fasting of the mass
Is enough to round out the signals
Of carriers
And all that is want to divest

The strangest dream

When love is at hand
Meaning becomes a scramble
And the tethers that bind
Are what we ought to see

But come now
Is there more?
More?
Is there a chance at it again?
Yes there is

And here
Where sand is between this vestige and the next

A City Sky at Night

There will be an undeniable thunder
That will not languish
For any person in the polish
Of this wooden frame
And the next
Be what may
I will come for you

What is longer?
And more of a vestige than a delight?
Here we see the vantage
Of all that will come to pass
The solemn rite
That spring deplores
Has missed the open tomb
That has as its bark
The rank and file
And here
Where we believe ourselves
To be the withholding of mass
There will be a coming
Of certainty
And the offerings of a thousand years
Will be tainted no more
We will live in solemn acceptance
And be that as it may
We will accept
The rite of spring
As a guide and lead only
And here
Where we find ourselves again
We will move again
Into the night
And through
And indeed
Beyond

Venom and Faust
That is our tale to tell
And here
Where the difference between the well
And the graveyard

Paul Fearne

Is all too near
I have a solution
That I will tell you only quietly
We are all
Already there
All we must do is look
And lo, it is found
Lo, it is found
The furnace and the gun
The life and the living thought
Is like a Paddington station trip
Through the lights of Parnassus
And into the dream
We come
And in this motion
Rise up
For the ready-ness
And the all

The sight of many a ship
Puts blinds on my soul
And hearts on my weeps
And when we come again
There will be a chance
To be the stranger in the night
And revel in this status
As the harbinger of solitude
Be the one
To test the waters
Be the one
To state on one side
Be the one
To fall into the pool
And then swim the Hellespont
Just to show
You can do it too
And here
Where the can meets the eagle
There much time for rejoicing
And all the time
And wealth of fun and happiness
For all time

A City Sky at Night

Is had
And then had again

What have we to say?
When shards of being-less is a fronting
And the nuance of the reminder is here
Loss of the duty is abundant
And the lamb is here
But where is the studio?

In the middle of random lines
There is sense
We only must talk it through
And here
Be the ones who shine
We will never let go
Of the changing of the guard
And then
When we seek no more
There will be release
And a whole lot more besides
What is left
Is nothing we can speak of
What is left
Is always what we speak of

There was a moment
I thought it was real
But it was a ghost
That has no corporeal sense

What this is to do with life, I don't know
And in the middle of it
I cry out
And know myself to be a feather in your bow

And now
When we sleep
There is time to weather the storm
Of lost condolences
And that is sparked
In times of wanting stress

Paul Fearne

And desire laden fruit
And when we see ourselves
In the deepening our well
We will know what is
And what can be
And here
Where we list from side to side
There will be a run of the mill again
And all that will come to pass

Be sure in yourself
That is all I can teach you
And when you are through
Wham
A fathomable desire
And then
The wish is there

What is more in tune than this?
What has the feathers of a thousand nights labour?
What endures despite it all?
I can answer all of these
'What is more in tune than this?'
Any book in the western cannon
'What has the feathers of a thousand nights labour?'
The eagle, of course
And
'What endures despite it all?'
You and me

And there we go
The answers to life's questions
All wrapped up
And here
Where the dance is at its ebb
We will float dreams down the river
And know it to be a strong current
But what of us now?
Where are we, now the dream is floating past
Do not talk is such a fashion
We have the dream it is ours
And no one can take it

A City Sky at Night

But we must allow for reality
And then
Back to our dream!

Gaining in momentum
I stand to salute fate
I love this
The too and fro
Of all that is
I am a writer
And must believe in fate
It travels through me
And in me
And out of this thing that is the most high

There are times
When we sit
Under the bower of the night
But we must not remain there
We must fight
For all that is
And in fighting
We will carry ourselves away
Into the depths
And the heights
Into what awaits
And through
And everything!

What is there here?
Does death lurk around these ivory cornices?
I have no time now
To see what is in the dark
I have only the vision
To keep me company

In line with these thoughts
I see the company travelling
There journey is one of mist and song
And here
Where we need more to escape than to tread
There is a noise

Paul Fearne

What is it?
It is us
As we travel
Between this birdcage and the next
But what do we see
Here and there?
It is us
As we travel
Once again
Through the night
And into what awaits
Be sure
It will come
But not now
(which is a blessing, and not a disguise)

There are times for change
And times not
But in the ever changing world
There is one constant
And that is change

What I have
Is the gist of it
And here
Where I need myself to be
I will fathom the impossible
And know it to be a thing of beauty

Come now
We must not shirk our responsibility
We must be in line with fate
And have as our sounding buoy
All the sages
Past and present
I have read them
Not all
But enough
And now I must fight
As if fighting is a thing done in the past
And here
Succeed

A City Sky at Night

There is no hope in the slap-dash
We must deliberate
Until the moon travels over the horizon
Yes the horizon
The deep beyond
There is more
Here
Than we ever had hoped

And when we are through
There is a noise
It is the noise of ages
As she comes in quick-succession
In this noise
Is the world
We see our past
And know it to be a trump-card
That will outweigh the rest

The difference
Between the sign
And the mighty
Is not too dissimilar
To the race
And the course

What is this thing
Which we bury in due course?
It is the loadstone
And the vector
And all that seems inordinate
What is the semblance of the night?
Where does it come from?
And where does it rest?
We have not come for harvest
We have come for tea
And here
Where we beckon oh so dear
We will relinquish something of note
And something that does not steer
But here

Paul Fearne

Oh here
Where the deliverance is not on the wind
There are chances to be
And chances to believe
Once again
That life is here
And the newness of the sonnets breath
Is not what can be said

The catchment of our hearts
Is more than enough to bare
And here
Where love flounders on rocks unbroken
There will be time for remorse
To undertake its noble journey

What we have
In the meantime
Is the weather of things
As they charge unto the moisture
And are seen dry

The momentum of an avalanche
Is here in the offing
We will catch its rays
As if the time had only come to be
I am the one who feels
Without feeling
But this is not the only way to travel
There can be things to do
And places to be

But here
In the afterglow
There will be heart
And soul
And,
Well yes

What is love?
It is the sunlight
It is the moon

A City Sky at Night

It is the tumult
It is the longing
It is all we feel
But more
Than the sum
Of its parts
Be the charge
Of horses reared
And you will feel it
As if nothing had gotten in your way
Here we stand
On the precipice of the unknown
But it is known
Not like this
Be sure you are ready
It will cost us dearly
But when we are through
Rest
And respite
In due course
My love

The weather
In this part of the world
Is more than we have been used to
And here
Where the newness of a fading sun
Is enough to be the light
Of a thousand ships
And a thousand ways to be

Be in tune with it
And the noise of the multitude
Will no longer ring in your ears

Have the way home clearly marked
And the din of the sea
Will only be the thing that announces
Your partnership with the world

What do we do to sleep?
We gather our clothes

Paul Fearne

As sit them on our lap
Then under the blanket
And then dream a dream of acceptance
And away we go
We never remember our dreams
But in them
We live

We come
In the night
And see ourselves as wraiths
But what we find
When the light of the dawn finally emerges
Is that we are there
Where we want to be

But come now
Is this it?
I have fathomed much in my time
But I have not fathomed this

When the rain comes
We move
Another step closer to the centre
I write for you
Oh blessed one
You are blessed with the strength to carry on

And here
Where the moisture rises
There is a time for respite
And a time to be once again
But in a different form

The seething mass
I see it
Until it rains its shards upon me

The semblance of the night
Is here
But I have won an important victory
And that is here

A City Sky at Night

And now

I sense more to come
But what of the world?
I hear it
It screams vast tentacles
And then laughs at the swirling

I am not one to be frowned upon
But still
The mass exists

There is time
Here
Amongst the tangles
To lay a vast wreath
And when we come
There will be nothing to stop us

 What do we see
When we look
Ahead
We see flowers
Rain
A rainbow
And then
Togetherness
And the ripening of old age

And here
Where the constant is to change
There will be laughter
And a fair amount of cheer

No not languish
There is no time
There is no time
For the wanting of the sun
For its birth
For its death
For all its saving of
And all its reluctance

Paul Fearne

The tutelage of the stars
Will be here
Soon enough

What is this left?
The sands that burn
And the shakes that shake
And here
Where the noise of our grandfathers sleeping
Is enough to wake all of us
We see
The fires that sustain
For what they really are
There will be an avalanche of forgiveness
And all that is wont to pass

The tender hooks
Of the night time escapade
Is the same as a wanton board
That believes itself enamoured
By all that will come to pass
What is here
Oh life?
What is there
Oh life?
We are it
In a nutshell
We are the ones who will be
And being true
Will fathom
All that is most dear
Again
And again
Yes

What is left of us
When the sand has shifted?
It is nothing other
Than all
And here
Where we saddle up to fate

A City Sky at Night

There will be a chance to breathe
A new breath

The truth of us
Is written in silk
I have nothing left to give
Only the silence
That has as its partner
The semblance of the night

I am unlucky in many things
And this is one of the them
But I say to you
Do not believe
But only in the all

The sense we have
To carry on
Is a fire stick
That heralds all new days

The wanting we have to be free
Is nothing other
Than our own self
As it wanders here and there

What we say
When we have a tongueful

When we come to the right place
Here we sit
And meditate on bygone eras

The sense in the trees
Is nothing other
Than our own sense

What we find
When we feel

There are truisms
And there is fate

Paul Fearne

We will say more

And here
Where we are left to the sun
We will find new voice
There is nothing more tremendous
Than this

The victory is won
The tables are cleared
And when we saunter
There remains a thing diminished
By all the weight
And that is me
But I am back
This much is sure

Be the wanna be's
And then turn your back
There is more to be said
That the lark can ever savour

What is this?
Stored?
It is life
In all its admittance

There is enough here
To fill what remains
The tightness
Of the sense of camaraderie
Is entirely warranted

What we see in the cracks
Is what we have always known
And here
Where the night beckons
I will have love
And all that will bring

The kindness of a star

A City Sky at Night

Fills the void
And when we are at the precipice
There will be longing
And a little bit of regret

What coaches us through these times
Is our own inner voice
It is there to guide us
And not to do ill

The chimes of the clock
Are now ready
For us
And our departure

When the sun sings
I will be here
Where the life beckons
I will treasure
There can be nothing more than this

And when we find ourselves in times of trouble
We can look back
On these golden years
And see them to indeed be a thing of beauty
This much is written
On all the parchment
Of all the manuscripts
That have ever been written

Here
We where we find ourselves
Without time
There is a truncated rhythm
That spurs us on
And knows that in each fledging
Is a greater flying
This flying
Is neither
Here
Nor there
But forever upwards

Paul Fearne

And through

There can be no finer thing than this
To be here
During fate
To see the tassels of the morn
And to see them flourish
This is the most gracious thing

And when we see through
To the end of life
We will see a mighty concurrence
That seems an ablution
But is more than life can bare

The testament
Is in the wiring
And when we see fit
We will launch on tables unknown
And we will couch ourselves in letters
And know duty to be a coachmen

There seems too much in the convent
To stay
So we will give ourselves
That space, and more

There is travesty
Amongst the clouds
They gather to run amok
Amongst the sky

The sentience of the sky
Is more than a mere play
It sends arcs and traces
Into fledgling mass

Do this thing
In whatever you do
Be kind
And the world will look after you
Be the standing

A City Sky at Night

And you will stand alone
Be the weather
And it will guide you
Do not be inclement
It will not suit you

There are times we should miss
And times we should gain
And in this there is life
Life as we never thought

What we thought was our demise
Has turned into a gate
An aperture to the sublime
That sees us through
And into
And out

The comingling of starry nothings
Is all that keeps us here
And when we say our greetings to the dawn
There will be more than nothing
Much more

Sing in hope
And sing with pride
There is nothing to hold us back
Nothing to launch us into the water
And back again

What we say to ourselves
When we feel the rush of togetherness
Is more than the rhapsody in blue
Will ever conquer

And when we see ourselves
For what we truly are
Here there will be laughter
And not so much belief

 The distance we now cover
Has the fawning mass to decree

Paul Fearne

It was wont to be kind
Which stood it in good stead

And when we fathom the bottom
Of this worn out intensity
There will be life
And all that it will bring

The song is one of play
The song is one of sensitivity
And when we sing
We sing for us
We sing for the world
And the newness of a fading light

What we don't have is ease
This is a myth
Any person
Who sings in the throng
Is like the rainbow
That has a clean in need

What we say
When we leave
Is never enough
Just to be

And when we cast a look at the sky
One last time
Here we will finally know the truth of our thoughts
And we will see them burgeon
Into things unseen

What we cast
Is the dye of remembrance
And here
Where we have time
We see things past
And things present
And things future
In what is left of us
Polish!

A City Sky at Night

And persistence

There is never more than enough
Enough is enough
And that much said
We go on
And see ourselves in the door way
That frames love

We see ourselves
In the mist
We are glorious
In our splendour

What we see
In the middle of things
Is not our true selves

The distance
Between this raindrop
And the next
Holds all

The semblance of the night
Is not our night
Our night
Rests in light

The further we come
The further we steel ourselves
The adventure is all

And here
Were we stand
There is rain
Not of the sort you would imagine
But hard rain nevertheless

The sense we have to persist
Is like a mist
That covers all the ground
And is not dispersed

Paul Fearne

For any sun

I have in me
That fire
That does not burn

There are songs
That are not sung
In the middle
Of any recourse

And here
Where the fire
Is at its peak
I will not rest
For any thing
Or any body
I will gather myself
And know respite

The thing that lives
Is the thing that binds
To this condition
Or the next

We fight
And not in vein

And when we are through
A lasting bit of the real
To know our forebears by

And the dance
Is one of solitude
These halcyon days
Are the thing that lets us sleep

And now
In the interim
There is good news
Of once that was lost
And now returned

A City Sky at Night

We further ourselves
Until there is nothing left

The sense we have
To continue
Is like a breeze in an autumnal land

And here
I see things clearly
I know not when to stop
But what is it worth?
This drive
It is the earth
As I am the sun
And now
Where we catch a glimpse of things
There will be a new need
To straddle the stars
And all that they will be bring

A belief
That's it!
A simple belief
In what is to come
That will see me through
And above
And beyond

Be the thing that never gives up
This is key

What is there left
Of the sky?
It is here
In our embrace

The noise gathers pace
But we will not let it carry us
When we are here to do business
And all that will bring

Paul Fearne

The noise
The noise
It is there
On a distant mountain peak
We will not languish for it
For a moment
We will see the clouds
And then chase them before us
Like gulls for a child

The next best thing
In the armoury of forever
Is now the time
It hears us
As we travel
And are ignited

And now we write
Like never before

There has never been a time like this

And now
On the firmament
We see ourselves
In mighty garb
It is here!
Oh mighty one
It is here!

And then
When the stars are worn out
We will have more time than ever
To feel our way through things
And here
Where the dust has not settled
There will be
A place for all of us

The gust of wind that brought me here
Has left
But what remains

A City Sky at Night

Is nothing other
Than
Totality

I have sensed a new dawn
It opens to catch me
And sends me flying

What is this?
I have found my mark
It is the wound that gathers
Me into a new dust

Hang onto yourselves
There is something more
There is something to see
Here
It is the west wind
But how do we see that?
Look to the trees
They will tell a story

And then we were there
Just waiting amongst the mass
Seeing ourselves gathered
And then
Well just
Then

I write
Like never before
I sing
As if in a trance
I dance
On the embers of fate

And when the song is enriched
There lies hope
And in hope
There is truth
And when the sands of this hourglass
Are empty

Paul Fearne

There will be much to do

The tempest is a withholding
That snares the temptress in gold
And when we see ourselves
In morning mist
There will be time
To hear ourselves
In the echo of the afar
As it heralds a new dawn
And a new way to be

The distance
Between
This raindrop
And the next
Is enough to fill our souls
To the brim

And here
Where we gather pace
We need something to tether us
What will this be?
The nearby willows
Will have the answer
I will ask them

And now
Before we have begun
There seems nothing to stop us
And here
Where fountains reign supreme
We will gather our selves
Until new tidings prevail
And then withstand no more

The emptiness of the range
Comes to this adventure
But what has been usurped
Is nothing new

And the range

A City Sky at Night

Is not enough
It fears to tread
Where I have gone

I have developed the formula
It will take me there

And when we are at rest
This is where we do our best work
We think about many things
And they oblige

What has the temptress in store?
Are there things of other worlds?
Are stones of fathomless seas?
There are new things
And old
And all that we thought
Would pass the test

And the angels sing
And we are through
Take rest

There is verily enough
To quench the young man's thirst
But here
Where the sands of the hour glass
Boast a new time to tell
There will be a toast
To any man's will

The hole in the window
Was not there to begin
Instead
There was a crack
That ran down the middle of it
And when we sing
A new song
There will be hope
But not for the adventure of the now
Here

Paul Fearne

There is a mighty becoming
A new way to be
And a new solstice to achieve

The park bench
Is where we sit
And here
The marrow runs thick
Unto climes of glass
And urbane misanthropy

The tempest in the sink
Is like
Water for the gulls
What is more
There will be no time for acceptances
We are too rushed

And here
Where thousands of nightly gulls
Bask in sea's light
There will be a chance
To have it all
One last time

The never ending ride
That I have embarked upon
Is not something to mock
I will not hear it
Until it is over

The withstanding of sound
Is all we fight for
What have I won
But all
What have I found
But all

What is there left?
There is the sun
As it casts its light
There is the wind

A City Sky at Night

That bares nothing
There are the clouds
That feel themselves wanted
And what is more
There is life

But what is life?
It is here
It is now
It is the fore longing
And the night
It is what keeps us
Until there is no more
And even then
What do we do?
We gather ourselves
And know things will be short

Do not be dismayed
There is more time
Than we ever thought possible
What is it that we say?
Is there nothing more than this?
There is
In a sense of speaking
A place that heralds all dawns
And in this place
There are dreams lived
But not forgotten
There are happenings
That know no ilk
And when we come there
There is no foreboding
But what is this place?
It is us
As we live
And breathe
And have all the hands above us

There is no time to shirk
There is only time to feel
And when we are through

Paul Fearne

A mighty release
That comes as an avalanche
That does not known when to stop

And here
In the break away
There is breakfast
And aplomb

I am new to this
This chance at being
I have had
In my time
Many a wanderings
But this is by far the best
I have set my sights on the future
But the now is so full
I have wantings that jar
But not enough to gather pace

I will be the one who says
'yes, and then, yes'
And here where we lament
Our never before glimpsed homecoming
There will be no time to see ourselves
In all our glory

Be the time
It will suit you
Be the place that beckons
And all of it will be yours
This can never be what we are after
We have more flamboyance that a mare
And then some

This is the sea
This is the place to be
What we have
Is so much more
I am the wind
And the rain
I come to be a part of it

A City Sky at Night

And see myself from afar

There is no need
Like this one
There is no solace
Other than the feet of the great

Be the chance
And I will be the flame
Be the happening
And there will come a belief
That causes new feelings
And more besides

The distance between
This acceptance
And the nearing at hand
Is a glimpse we must have

This is it
Love and loss
I have the formula
That will take me there

There is so much I must do
But I will not waver

The sense we have
That things will right themselves
Is the feeling of us all

The dimensions of this world
Cannot contain the deliverance

What is more
I am free
I love the journey
As it loves me

Be the tempest
As you love to be

Paul Fearne

The sense in the hills
Is no sense at all
But a wonderful deliverance

There is no time like now
To feather our bows
Bows of hope
And bows of joy

Be the time
And you will have a great victory

This is the want
And the dream
Of all those who have gone before us

The feelings we have
For the past
Are no more
They linger
But are not of this station

Be in time
And the newness of a fading sun
Will be all we want

There are now influences
That defy description
But despite this
Somehow we will win!

What we say
And what we believe
Leave their mark

I am here
Like never before

The silence does not ring

When we come
There is life

A City Sky at Night

When we leave
It leaves also

The fathoming
Of autumn gulls
I will come for you

This is my want
And my feeling

I sense a great thing
It comes
And I am ready

What we believe

This is it!
The semblance of tomorrow
The dream
The want
The invective
The sense
The desire
The following
The hence
That knows no sense

Where does poetry take us?
It takes us to the beyond
And back again
Around
And through
And towards
Back again
And around again
Through the mist
And to the top of every mountain ever climbed
This is it
I know it
And here
We will find rest
And that little bit of respite

Paul Fearne

That we all want

This is it!
I have made a grand discovery
I have always known it
I have always used it
But it is here now
In great torrents
To suffer
And create
This is the formula

But what of the night?
She has no movement
Except for a starry cloud
That moves around her

The distance
Between this raindrop
And the next
Is a well-spring we must not forget

Be in tune
And troubles seem distant
And here
Where we live
We will find more
Than we had hoped

Take a gathering from the harvest
And spread it far
Take your own hand
And shake it
You have done well

We will know
When we are through
That times are here for changing
I write
Only because it is a compulsion
I live
Only because I can

A City Sky at Night

And here
Where love is still persistent
I catch myself
And know grace and airs
That believe themselves true
In the mist of time
And the cavalcade of remembrance

Be that which may
And time will come to you
It will bring sweet fruits
And the time it takes

I hear you
You are near
But in the meantime
I sit
And wait

But what is this
Seething through the mist
It is dawn
She comes
And I wait

The nearest post
Is the simplest
It comes
Like we never thought we were

And here
Where the sun beats the loudest
I will not deny myself
I will come for deliverance
And know it to be a trance

The thing that keeps me
Is the sound of longing
I long
And know that the day will have its fill

Paul Fearne

The day is long
As the night is short
But what carries us
Is not the same thing
That throws us away
These two things are different
And they follow us
As night turns into day

The momentousness of my task
Is one of beauty
But I will tackle it surely
With utmost virility
And here
Where things seem strange
I will come
And not shirk back
I will come
And know my task to be achievable

This much is said
But what is unsaid?
The tenacity of the day
That is what

What do we see
When darkness falls?
We see ourselves
As we come for fate
The new need we have
To straddle the stars
Will be enough to get us there

And when the time has elapsed
There will be something of the unexplained
Something deep within us
That carries forth
And does not submit

It is here that we tarry
It is here that we ride
On that dragon of insistence

A City Sky at Night

The night is nothing other than a farce
It bears all
But does bely its fate

And when we sing for the new dawn
There comes a warning
We must not wait for acceptances
We must come now
And be true to ourselves

I am writing for all of us
This much is true
I know that when the gates are open
We must not avert our gaze
For here is the semblance of what has been
And what will be

The new stain on old fabric
And here
Where we wish to be
There is nothing to keep us

The thing that is said
In night
Is not the same
As the thing
That is said in day
But here we tarry
And know nothing else

The distance we shed
Is not bright
It is dull
And in need of care

But what we cannot do
Is fathom a new sense
Of the old
And then some

And now we have it
There is silk

Paul Fearne

Where jam had spread

And now we give ourselves to the moon
And see where that will take us

It is never ending
This ride
Never ending in the fortitude of it all
I catch a glimpse of myself
And there is only the spark
Of all or nothing passion

What must I do?
To find the levity
Of another dawn
Am I encumbered
With a drizzle of salt
And mouth piece of forever

There can only be one way
And that is through

What belongs to the night?
It is here
Shedding light

What is the notion of the stars?
They are here
Despite ourselves

What do we say is with us?
All that is

What can we be?
We can be all

There is derision in the mist
It knows not which way to turn

There is suffering here
Suffering there

A City Sky at Night

And through it all
We hang tough

Through it all

And together

What shall fall?
The healing mind
Or the grip that sustains

Here
That is the placate-able
And in the morning
Silence

I hear the sound of the wind
It comes in magnanimous portions
But will we ever see it?
I think not

And then
When we least expect it
The turning of fingers on grass
That will be a sustained fibre
That rings through the ages

Love me
Not for who I am
But for what I be
And then I challenge you
Leave
And be not gone
There will be more
I grant you

I find you tethered
To a rock
But this is not for me to undo you
You must escape
But you will not
So here we sit

Paul Fearne

At the crossroads
Welling up to the ages
Leaving marks of the mighty
And finding a champion in the wind

What is there left of us?
Nothing that can be sustained
What have we thought is all?
There will only be the rye
The smile and the compunction

The wanting is here
We do not believe it
We hear mighty dreams
In the back of our heads
This much will come for you

Do not be a surgeon in this place
Be a lark
And you will lay bark

What can we say?
Is there ever a need to stay?
This is more that we know
And more than we hoped

The distance that envelopes us
Is not the same as the eagle
As it fly's to ancient heights
Be the oracle
And you will win
Every race
Put to you
By every runner
On every fence
On every corner
Of any street
And here
We must call an end to it
It bleeds as it runs
And has to much invective
The stammer is a curse

A City Sky at Night

But we overcome it
For the good of things
And then
Belief
And all that will come

The sense we all have
To dive into it
Is the way of all greatness

And when we charge our glasses
A great release

And now
In the meantime a weather
We wait
And are consoled

What is this thing
That comes?
Should we be a part from our loved ones?
To view it
Yes
And no
Be patient
And be wise
There will come a time for belonging

And now
When we see things clearly
There will be dust to settle
And people to greet

I have one way
And that is up
I have one way
And that is up and across
I have one way

And now
In the meantime of the letting go

Paul Fearne

There will come a new song
That launches into life
Like a new found commiseration

The sense we have
To still the core
Is what we have been doing all along
And now
When the fruit of our labours
Is coming in droves
We will find ourselves in the midst of it
One more time

And now
There can be no more of the carrier pigeon
We are here
To do as we like
But what of the sky
That turns around a tender earth?
Is it the one that seeks?
Is it the one that has the rye on the ground?
There is never enough to settle this
And here
I languish
But wait
I live!
I live, and surely my death is a way off!
But this is not enough to say 'aplomb'
It curls in time
And with a whisper for its name
We come for the dawn
But stay for the accoutrements
The nestling of all the stars
And all the wantings
That ever lived
Are now in the board room of forever

And come
There comes a quick
It ceases to be made
And longs to be fed

A City Sky at Night

I hinder not
But transpose the teleology of the stars
And here
Where there can be nothing of note
I fawn again
And write!

What is the day
But a misnomer?
What is the night
But a nomer?
And here
Where longing has its fill
There can be no more
Of this
Or that
Or all
Or nothing
The throw of the dice
Here we find stillness

I love the way
We stand
We stand together
And have our fill

And now
Quietude
And a wanting to be sure

There is a chance here
That we will make it
But before then
The hard road
It is a road of broken dreams
And lost souls

But here
Oh here
There is enough to placate us
I have sensed

Paul Fearne

More than my share
I have believed in things like they were
Be the one who willows
And you will find the embrace

What have I left?
But all that is
What have I felt?
But the wind
There is more here
Than we had hoped

This is what we have come for
A new need
A new want
A new desire to be the best we can be

And here
Where the distance doesn't matter
We live
And breathe
And have our souls
Transmuted to gold

I am the one
Who has the right to sing
I believe
In many things
I see
What was foretold

The treasure is in our hearts
And minds
And bodies

And then
When we least expect
A new beginning
And all that will come to pass

There is no time
To do the things which count

A City Sky at Night

There is no time
To finish what must be finished

But here
Where we stand
A thousand breathes await
But this is not the issue

What we have
Is a thousand nights sleep
That ring in the ears
Of all who travel

I am comfortable here
As I write
But what we say in the dream time
Is enough to wake

The distance of the musings
From life
Is never apparent

We will have fun
This life and I

There is no time
But the distance is here
Already

I believe that we may be the dawn
As the sunset is the way
I believe we may have the day
Just as the night is the form

Have a might
In the face of togetherness
Have a song
At your lips
As the tune is like an ember

The sighing of winter roses
Is not enough

Paul Fearne

To be what we need
To gather the weeds
That distil the sorrow
Of all that is
And all that will be

I have no need
Now
For anything
Only this
As we rise once again
Onto pinions
Of deliverance

There will be a time
In the not too distant future
Where I will be in amongst the petals
But until then
I write

There is a way that has no encounter
With all that is
But this is long
And with care
We will be

The drawn and the packaged
Will be my invigoration
And when I am through
The life of the day
Will be a blessing

The silence in the night
Is all we feel
I do things
To write
I do things to be
And here
Where we have the newest of the new
There will be a song
On the lips of ever sailor

A City Sky at Night

There is no error here
Things happen
And things release
What we try for
Is nothing short of all

But the journey is not the respite
The journey is the respite
I write
Please let me write
I write
And am placated

The beauty of the mountain pass
Is enough to draw me ever onward
But here
Where the sound of broken glass
Is enough to still
I will have it
Like never before

And now
When I sit
And write
I write for you
Dawn
And no one else
I sit for the things that come
I sit for the day break that has no sheen
I sit
And believe once again
That life is virtuous

The longing I feel
Sits true
It is sense I have always had
In the night
I dream
That is true
But no longer remember my dreams
I hunt
But have a hunting amnesia

Paul Fearne

I sing
But to nobody

There is the here and now
I long for it
But have more than my fair share

A new dawn
Has opened
And here
Where time has its presence
There is nothing left to do

I have had my say
And now there
Is more to do
Than ever
I sit
And am consumed
I write
And them am immersed

The gaining of momentum
Is in the sense of things

And here
Where we have loved the most
There is time for the movement to gather pace
And now
When we live hardest
A new change
A gentle change
One that will startle
As it builds

Be true
The wind is here

What we have said
Cannot be unsaid
What we have been endeared by
Is in the mist

A City Sky at Night

And when we talk
There is a litter
A litter of a thousand souls
We know now that talk is strong
But what is stronger still
Is life

Be the tempest
And I will be your gale
Be the way
And there will be nothing left to say

There comes a time
That blisters as it unleashes
And here
Where we find ourselves
There is the newness of a work of art
It sprinkles
As it barks

 The mist
The mist

The sense we have
That the dawn is here
Is more than just a sense
It is a great intuition
That harbours all

Be in the middle
Of this and that
And you will find yourself strong

What we say
When the light fades
Is nothing more than all

The happiness we sometimes feel
Is not us
It is the world's
As she shines debris of every colour

Paul Fearne

I have found the way
It is in the walk
Of a thousand sailors
Who never look back

There is nothing here
But the backyard to the beyond

There is a sound
That harbours no fear
There is a fear
That harbours no sound

I have the dream
I have the sense
I have the nonsense
And here I will stay

There can never be anything grander than this
To be tethered to fate
And have my hands swinging

I love the sound
As it pulls me
It pulls me to that ancient place
That place beyond the hills
And into what awaits

I will write through this
And know that I am raised

The dimension of things
Far outstrips the need
The dimension of things
Is the need

We have come far
But how much further can we go?
There are trees that dim
And trees that light
But the fight

A City Sky at Night

The challenging fight

The listening we do
To stave off time
Is enough to quench our thirst
How big will this be?
It will be big enough

As I have said
I have the formula
But what is most in need
Is time
Can we make it?
Yes we can

Has the wind blow?
Or is it still here?
I think it has blown!

The night time in which we sleep
Has brought dreams of calm
The restful dream
But what of the rest of us?
We have no way of finding out

Intuition
That is the key
Intuitions that burble truth
That is all we can go on

And here
Where the wind is a misnomer
There will come fragments
To tide us

And when we sleep
GREAT dreams
Dreams of further longing
That steel themselves to rocks of clay
Be the thing that binds
And you will have your work
Be the thing that tarries

Paul Fearne

And life is yours

I have the formula

What is more
I have life

And in this arrangement
Great things are done

But what of the now
We must say yes
A journey towards the now

I am one to fathom
I am one to be true
I am one
And in this one
Is the world

I languish on fates untold
I languish
On the riverbed
I languish
On the dreams of men
But there is more to say
So let us begin

There can be more to be with
There can be more to see through

And when we are done
A great sigh
A great wind
And a great solace

This is where we are at
This is dream and the want
And the nexus of untold desires

Be intimate with the world
It contains a great lesson

A City Sky at Night

Of un-satisfactoriness
And all that will entail

I have a need
To be without wings
But I have them
And they are with me
I fly to close to the sun
My wings are wax!

But this is how we fly
Always too high
And always too low

There are chances
When it rains
There are beliefs
That do not falter

In the middle
Of it all
I find solace
It comes
In spits and spats
I write
To soothe the pain
Of a thousand nights labour

In the sense we have
Between nonsense
There is light
There is light
Like never before

Here comes the train
It is laden
With all who come to pass
The pass
Yes the pass
There is time

What have we got

Paul Fearne

But all that is
What will we be
But all that is

I am a well-spring
That heads no advice
I live on the hills
And in the trees
And know that life is a miracle

Be sure
This much I ask of you
Be sure
And the telling of roots of ancient trees
Will be enough

There is tension here
But it is now gone
I love to whistle in embers of delight
And know that sentient skies
Will have their fill

The whistling we do
To pass the time
Has a new way to be
It will never end

There are changes here
More than I ever could have imagined
I have had the distance
Now I have the heart

Fathoming
I call it
Where we collide in ancient wonder

Be the life
And all will be yours

The fellowship of clouds
Has a dimension
I have not seen for an age

A City Sky at Night

Try not to be
Anything you don't want
Try and be
All that you can

I have heard
In this seeming rainbow
A noise
That comforts
As it cajoles

Shall we say
The moon is a godsend
And the stars
Trailers into infinity
The clouds?
A herald to the day
What we find
When we look
Is nothing short of all

The final say
Is here
And we have come out on top
Only because of luck
And a new found longing

Be at the ready
It will give you much

And here
Where sand is like rose petals
There will be a long fought for release
And unheralded day

There is a wholesome mist
That is preparing to depart
Similarity in difference
Is what I once preached

Paul Fearne

And now
When the wind has died down
And the shadows are no longer a part of us
We will find new voice
And new machinations
To believe by

The tenacity of each fawning breath
Is here now
I no longer succumb
To my fate
As I once did
I only succumb to the embers of time
That travels deep in anticipation
Of all the is here

Belief
We believe
And are washed
Of every fibre that once contained us
And now
Newness
And a little encompassing

It is nice
To feel this way
I am comfortable
And at ease

But the mist still brings
A new found acceptance
And here
Where we have votive strength
There is a nice sound to it all
And new found well-wishes

The dream
It is strong
It does not languish
Nor diminish

What we had thought was the finish

A City Sky at Night

Is a new beginning
What we though was the end
Is another chance to strive

Be what may
There can only be one outcome now
And that is through
And out
And never in between

What we see
When we see no more
What we feel
When the race is here to be won
There are solstices
And then there swimming races

And here
Where we find our calling
There is enough to be free
And here freedom
Has no cost

The tendrils of another dawn
Are waiting
They will see, in themselves, a vantage point
A point from which to see
The whole world turning

And then
When we have had enough
A visage
And all that can be transcended

Where is there to go?
Where is there to be?
The life goes on
But the sand is no more

What we thought was a hurricane
Is nothing other than our thoughts

Paul Fearne

What we insist upon
Is that ruptures in the fabric
Be tuned to the right pitch

And here
Where we fathom the hardest
There will be new chances
And old ways

Come now
We must not forget
We have come so far
But what is left of the journey?
It is all here
And there
And everywhere

The small things count
And the big things
Well they count to

There is never more solace
Than when writing
This is the law of the code
And the code of the people

Be the one who laughs
Your vision is set
The tangential remains of the cistern
Will guide you home

I can write what I like
And I will

That is enough to take me
Where I want to go

There is a logic to it all
But it is not us for the understanding

I come
And am treasured

A City Sky at Night

And do not fall

Here we go!

The next thing is something to hold
It comes
And is in need of the time

The steps along the way
Are hard
But we should not fear them
They bring solace
And some respite

The catch in the distance
Is not about us
It is about we
And there is a difference
If only semantic

The herald
That harks the breaking of the day
Is here now
Readying his instrument

The water we drink
Is enough to fashion a new boat
A boat with no oars
Only sails

And then, yes
We have it

I have no time
Like the present
I have no way to see
What is left behind

What can we say
When we see the debris
Of a thousand nights longing?
We see the morning

Paul Fearne

And the dusk
And all that has come to be

There are no snakes in the grass
Only red ink
On pale skin

The seeming impossibility of all this
Is written on the palms of every sailor
Who ever sailed the sea

And when we leave
We leave broken hearted

The impossibility of love
The clatter of hooves
The rifling of sound
We look
And lo there it is!

The driftwood in the sand
Tells an ancient fable
Of lands discovered
And then are requited
The distance doesn't matter
Here
Only here

The mass is thinking
It takes its time
It gives advice
That no one takes
But here
Where the load of bushels sleep
There is a new need to rally
Unto solemn states

And when we are though
There will come a reaching
And we will all believe again
And be in tune like never before

A City Sky at Night

There is a cavalcade
In the heart of things
And here
Where sand runs cheap
There is a wind to stop all wind
There is a dance to stop all steps

And when we find ourselves a fresh
There can only be one appointment
An appointment to the grand vision
Of love and all of her ilk

Dimensions degrade all
And niceties inflame the world

Be the one who dances
And all will be made clear
Be the one who subsides
And there will be clear fun

Be in the dresser
And the sandbox of time will deliver
I cannot say more than is
It is in our hearts to deliver

I see you now
Floating
I see you now
Away in the distance
Be the one who laughs!
I dare you!

All far ahoy!
There are tremors in these trees
They bite the nimble headed
And send shards to sleep
Once again

The distance
Between this shard
And the next
Is like rain

Paul Fearne

On a Sunday afternoon
It leaves us wet
But still having fun

The sense we have
Not to rain
On anything
Or anyone
Is the same sense
That we have
To catch our fairy lights
And have them hang from venomous bastions

What guards the entrance?
Is it love?
Or sight?
Or love at first sight?
Who knows

There is nothing more to do
I wait
And am pleased with what I see
There can only be footsteps in winter
They listen
And I tread
I see now where the horizon begins
It is like a whetstone that knows no length
It is like a feeling that never departs
It is like you and me
As we sit here
Ready of the ship to come in

There was once a freighter
That carried no freight
All it carried
Where invisible kisses
From every country on earth
And then
When it had completed its journey
Circumnavigating the globe
It came to rest
Here

A City Sky at Night

In my arms

What is more
There are times that bind
And times that breathe
And when we find them
We will come to the light filled end
With greater confidence
And a greater need to be

When we say
'There is no life here'
We mean that
When the stars have aligned
And the nightingale has had its song
There rasps a stallion
That flitters across the stage
And here
Where the merriment of a thousand nights is upon us
We will come again
In mere form
And not in mere shape

The distance between you and me
Is not so great
The distance between us
And the stars
Is
Similarly
Not so great

So why do we suffer then?
Why do we have a heart that can be broken?
Why is there not more in this life
And not just the next?
It is an almighty mistake
Not even that
It could have been anything
This world of ours
It could have been anything
But it is this
And we must adapt ourselves

Paul Fearne

This is what we must do
It is here and now
This world
Let us share this facet
As our own
And get on with the business of living
And share a song on us

That is right

There is loss here
And the fibre of the day
I hope
In the depths of the dream
You are fine
In the depths of it
You are fine
And that your thought multiplies to the dimensions of the sun

And when we gather ourselves
For one last adventure
We see that the cavalcade of mist
Has scattered
And we can finally see clearly
The rain is coming down
The wind is biting
And the cold is like a waist coat
Tight
And in need of adjustment
But when we have become cognoscente of these things
They depart
And we are left with
A circle floating in the sky
Warmth beating down
And the clear sky all around

There is now
No more song
There is now
No more wanting
There is only this

A City Sky at Night

And this is life
And all the heralds sing of it
And all the plans for the future are here
And all the new people come
And all the old people come
And all that is new
And all that is old
And all that cannot be
Is here
With us
Wishing us well
On our journey
Wishing us safe passage
And all that will pass for flair

The listening we now do
Is heightened
It sees, and yes hears
But only in good measure
And when we are done
Ah, yes, that is the way of it
Coming in barrels of laughter
And co-mingling in all that is

What have we seen
But all that is
What have we been
But all that is
Where have we sailed
But everywhere
What have we done
But everything

There is noise in the attic
The mice have found a home
We will leave them
To have their life
And when the time is right
We will open the door
And let them free

The mattering of the world

Paul Fearne

Is here
The dryness of the pool
Is a pitter-patter away
And here
Where we find ourselves again
Light
And all that is

What do you say
When the fire is at its height?
You say – 'yes' – and then water is found
To douse the flames
But why should we douse them?
These flames
Maybe they are meant for greater things?
No
We douse
And are never worried about it
And so we shouldn't be

I sing now
Oh so loud
But what is this song for?
It is for us
The traveller's
Travellers through the world
Who are entangled in this or that
Mode of being
This or that tribulation
This or that mighty release

And now
I see it
It is there
And I am here

I search
And what do I find?
Nothing of note
Nothing of the special
And nothing of the day

A City Sky at Night

I sit
And now I rummage
Through ancient bags
That tell of pristine conditions
And laughter that has no knell
Be the one who laughs loudest
And you will be given a mighty gift
It is in us all to laugh like this
But only one will find the way
And win the prize

The taste for it
Has come
It sits with me
And I stroke it like a cat
I sense more of a need to come
Back from all this
And be the one who listens to the world
Once again

What is there
But this
What is there
But that
I have felt
In my wanderings
A new need
A new desire
To be all I can be
And wish for others
A happy ride

What is there
But faith
What is there
But fashionings of older things
What is there
But the distance we seek
What is there
But the now
That encompasses all
What is there

Paul Fearne

But the wish of a thousand sailors
To come home speedily
And then have rest
On secure land

What is there left
But all
What comes to us in times of need?
Fondness
I have let go
Of all this
And now know what it is like
To swim against the current
It changes things
This current
It changes all we have
Into one bright spark
And here
Where the windows of our hearts
Are further from the daylight hours
And further from anything that binds
And when we seek acceptance
And the journey ends
We come in fits and starts
And then
Rest
And rest again
And here
Alive we live
In the shadow of a large oak
In a castle by the sea
Here we live
And write
And find love
And all things

There is in this tide
A fellowship of the laden
And here
Where we seek the newness of a fawning sun
There will come sparks
Not of remorse

A City Sky at Night

But of fortitude
I have found that which will take me there
I have found the co-mingling of the stars
In depths of pure night
I have found that which the soothsayers
Look for
So ardently
I have found the way and the need and the want
I have not been dull in my journeyings
I have been alive
Like now

And here
In the midst of it all
I find happiness
Like a hand soaked in soap

Like a hand soaked in soap
This is what the hours say
But what do we say
A hand soaked in time
And not thyme
But time
And here
I sense you are near
You are the one who bequeaths the sun
You are the one who does not stop
Not for any thing
Nor anyone

But what do we say
When the time has reached its zenith
What do we say
When the time has not stopped
We come again
And again
And we charge right to the top
Down again
And around
Only to settle at the base of it all
And here
Find it all

Paul Fearne

And do what we may
In times of difficulty

There is never enough time
To do what we want to
There is never enough space
To hang the things we want to hang
But in this breath
In this solemn breath
There are dreams
Of setting sail
Of being in the mould
Of having the rest
To conquer the blue of the bluest sky
And when we have
All that we can have
There will a victory call
That transcends all calls
And there
Where we are most at ease
There will be more than is possible
In one heart beat
To the next

This much is certain
This much is true

There are new ways to be
And they are here

Pushing and panting
The way through is not so easy
But easier than it was
By halves

The nearness of us
Of we
Of the shallowness of the night
Is here
Is there
Is around
And through

A City Sky at Night

Can we not see ourselves
In the moment?
In the minute
Between drinks
What is more
We have that acceptance
So we see ourselves anew

Does everything work here?
I have to say it does
That is more like it
To go from the afar
To the never ending
That is a nice journey
I would say

And now that we have the sisterhood of stars
As our guide
There will be no stopping us
Nothing to stop racing thoughts
Of who knows what
Nothing to stop
The vans of togetherness
As they sing
And hoop
And holler

What is there left
Of the chains that bind
Nothing
And nothing else
Will be said
I can write
Yes, I can
And so what causes you displeasure?
Nothing like a ride in the dark
I channel the Romantics
And know them to be free
Of all that is
And all that will be

Paul Fearne

The castle door is not locked
We should stand next it
And look out to the sea
It is a beautiful sight
This view of the sea
The sea mist as it rises
The blue-green-grey of its movement
This castle has housed a thousand people
But now it is mine
And I look onto it
With great fondness
Here
And there
And roundabouts
I see the land
As it crashes into the sea
It is not ours to give, this land
It is the centuries
As they unfold
On brass fittings
And iron works
Sometimes
I hear the sound of longing
And know that I am home

The test
Is the water
The test is
On the land
The most we have ever fought for
Is here with us
So we know
What can be
And what can't be

The sense we have
To narrow out apertures
 Is the same sense we have to bring forth the barbs of the day
And have them come with us
And through us
And around us

A City Sky at Night

And now
When we sing
There is nothing left
Nothing left of our lives
As they hold firm in the firmament
Be the one
Be the two
Be the three
And then…
Run
And run

And run

A slight limp
Is what came
To the chance of things
But this did not stop us
We carried on
And made a raft
From a tea cup
And fashioned it to the sea
Like a bottom of a boat
And here
Where the sun fails to be
There will be a cool breeze
That ends as it begins
This much can be told from your tea leaves
And when
The distance is too much
We will gather ourselves
And reach the harvest by nightfall
And know that we have had a mighty victory
And here
Where daggers do not weep
We will find love
And all that will come to pass

There is a place
It is not named
And has no address
It is a place

Paul Fearne

That whispers the sound of longing
It knows where it is
But no one else does
It does not feel
But pulses
In translucent light
And here
Where great things are done
There is a chance to be again
Without the ford
Or the hurried step
Without the seed
Or the tenure

And here
Where sound is given a second chance
There will be a new step
It knows only one belief
And that is here
Where we all are now
And when the dance stops
Here we will go
To know again
That life does not stop

And here
Where we sit the longest
I have found
The truth of it
It is a lack
An effervescence
Of life
Of the here
And the now
And the spectacle
That barks in dreams of day
Here
I surrender to you
And know you to be
That thing
That keeps going

A City Sky at Night

So now I wonder
What next
My goal is set!
And here I go
Towards the promised land
That tells no tales
And has no want

There is a place
In every heart
It beats as hard as iron
And dispels the mist
With joyous ease

And here
Where we sit for fun
Another adventure
Forwarding the last

And now
Where there is hope
I will not come to my self
With any ease or foreboding
The temptation is to relegate
This care
For the next

But in the chance we see
A larger forest
We see it now from the sky
But our trajectory is diminishing

Love
It is all that we can do

The difference between this moon
And the next
Is like a fabric of woven silk
It comes
And is not diminished

Paul Fearne

The withstanding of the cry
It loves
But does not hear
It follows
But has no ears to find

And true
What is lost in the semblance
Is not something we can stand
It treasures our need
But cannot be withheld

The test is in the strength
The test is the nightly embrace
I see you
But I cannot tarry
I love our banter
But there is no chance at what seems small

I am writing for us
To take the sense we have
And consume in the manner
We find appropriate

Sometimes there is sadness
Sometimes there is light
I have found the light
And always fear
That the day will not have me

There are times
When we fight
And in these times
There is a fierceness
It lingers
And matches on burnt wood

The dryness of my mouth
Is not enough to be the thing which delights
But here
Where the never ending ride
Has the sand at its finger tips

A City Sky at Night

There is life
And in that
We have our fortunes read
And know that we are safe
What is there
But the wind?
What is there
But the moon?
What are we
But all that is

I come
And am lifted
To that place amongst the hills

Be the one who does not shirk
Be the one who always wins
And here
Where love has built a nest
There will be times
To come

What we say
In the middle of our dream
I have found a way
It is here
Like the rest

The difference between sky's
Is enough to belittle the dawn
And here
We will sing

 I have known
Of many things
I have been the test
And the rule
I have been the verve
And the soil
In me lies the seed
I have seen it turned
I long for that

Paul Fearne

Which is in of my grasp

There is a funnel here
It circumnavigates the globe
And does not speak of oil
I love the life
But the life does not reciprocate
Only moments of abandon
Do I thrive

I live to be entombed
In this or that vault
But what we say when we see!
Ah, pure bliss

There is nothing that galvanises
More than this!

What have we come for?
Is it this, or that?
It is that
I knew it

This is not the shore
It is the aperture
I am at the height of my powers
I am not one to be
Only to see
And here
Where the mistletoe does not tell of an age
There will stand a new strength
It hums
And burns
And delights in its existence

Come again
We have not said too much
I hope
But in the meantime
Desire
And a pinch of salt

A City Sky at Night

I write
And release
And here
I fathom less than I ever have
But I write
So there you go

There is a thing
That is not gold
It is not silver
It sings
But is not of this earth
It believes in many things
But belittles nothing
And here
Where the dust settles
There is life
And all that it entails

I have found
The next adventure
It brings food
When it is needed
It delights
In all the small things

Come now
We must be hopeful

The mast head
Is overloaded
But that is not enough
To carry the wind
And the rain
Over another frozen ground

I have found which way to go
It is over hill
And dale
And when we strive for that little bit more
Here
The reactions to our song

Paul Fearne

Will be fixed in the firmament
And when we dance
Oh
How we will dance
The laughter will radiate
And clench in two sorts of first
The first being for the clouds
The second being for the ground
And here
There can never be anything more
Oh here
And when the sultan has decreed
There will be merriment
And all things dear

The desire to fly

What is left of the sand

What drives the ships over the sea

Hanging on, despite everything

Catching the last of our embers

The night and its entreaty

The sycamore lives on

The desire to see

What can only be thought in words

What has always been

The rail of fate

The wanting, and the needing

The high, and the low

A catching that surpasses

A City Sky at Night

Wanting to be the shore

Listening to all the day

A fixing that solves all

A new kind of being

What is left of the arc

There are times
When we should be the noise that accompanies fate
In this breath
Is the last of the vestiges
They come
In solemn mass
And believe in the time
That things are here for the keeping
Be the messenger
We will be
We will be
We will console
And then run the mile in a minute

There is now time
To see
What we want
To see
And here
Where the abyss yawns
We grow new wings
And off
And away!

The feather in our caps
Knows no indifference
It is a passionate thing
That has heart
As it has joy
And here

Paul Fearne

Where we perish
A thousand times
We write
And know that time will heal
And wounds will be softened

But in the meadow
There are buttercups
The sun shines
The dale does not diminish
And in the veracity of the times
New life
And older things

What is there left
Of our old life?
What is there to do
But get old?
I have fashioned a new type of thing
It bares no resemblance to any-thing
That has surpassed the age

And here
Where we speak of love and hope
There will come new direction
And old wares

Be the venom
And I will be your guide
Be the troupe and the circus will house you
Be anon
And on
And the treasures you seek
Will be cast upon you

The merriment of the day
Is like a four course meal
Bought to be savoured
And not estranged

 There are times
And when they come

A City Sky at Night

They flood
But here
Where we see ourselves in the mirror
There is nothing left to do

The wanting of fireflies
Encourages us
To reach for the firmament
Take a handful
And rise again

And now
Where things are seen closely
There is a new way
To be seen

Come and be a part of the grand adventure
It is if nothing has moved
It is as if
The solstice has not changed
In an aeon
Be prepared
It will serve you well

What have we left
That is not broken
What have we to do
That is not littered in shards

I will have the dawn
And I will see
Each day
With fresh eyes
And a heart that beats
And a soul that drums

Be the wind
I ask you
Be the sign
And you will have all

There can be no way to fathom this

Paul Fearne

Only in action
And reaction
Do we finally side up to the dream

Be the mountain
Yours will be a pass
Have dreams that are remembered
And you will have your fill

I see now
The distance
It is a thing that only comes lightly

Be in the seam
The seamstress won't mind

And when we are through
There will come greater things
Than ever was foretold in our combined dreaming

The newness of the sun
Is like a cold vacuity
It is tempered like never before

The well-wishes of strangers
Are enough here
To sell our outright post
And when we delight
The sands turn
And when we find ourselves again
There will be hope

Do not give in easily
Yours is the way

There can never be a chance
Quite like this one
There can only be sorrow along the way
But the goal is worth it

In the breeze
Lies a truth

A City Sky at Night

It is of you
And me
And all that we stand for
It comes
As a play thing
That knows no other way
There is much to be said
And much to do
About nothing
And everything
And all that lies in the dark

Be a kindness
The salt beckons
Be a dreamer
And clattering of cups will be yours

I have never been one
To love so cleanly
But what we do
Defines us

We have said so much
But now it is time
Time to fathom new branches
And believe once again
That it is all before us

www.ingramcontent.com/pod-product-compliance
Ingram Content Group UK Ltd.
Pitfield, Milton Keynes, MK11 3LW, UK
UKHW041412180426
11947UKWH00007B/76